The Birth of Undoing

ISBN: 9781963038422 .

The Birth of Undoing © 2025 Emily Patterson

Cover art: iStock photo: repinanatoly
Author photo: Devon Albeit

ISBN: 978-1-962405-30-0
Library of Congress Control Number: 2025940219

Sheila-Na-Gig Editions
Russell, KY
Hayley Mitchell Haugen, Editor
www.sheilanagigblog.com

The
Birth of
Undoing

poems

Emily Patterson

Sheila-Na-Gig Editions

Acknowledgments

Gratitude is given to the publications below, where many of these poems first appeared, sometimes in earlier forms or under different titles:

Autumn Sky Poetry DAILY: "Turning Thirty in Miami"
CALYX Journal: "Unearthed"
Cathexis Northwest Press: "Periphery"
The Christian Century: "I Sit Among the Mothers"
Free Verse Revolution: "Anniversary at New River Gorge," "From Forest to Sea," "Walking in the Rain I Wonder When Postpartum Depression Becomes Just Regular Depression"
Heartburn Review: "Ultrasound"
The Magnolia Review: "Mother of Mine"
Minerva Rising Press: "On the Playground, I Think about How a Mother Is Like a Moth"
Mom Egg Review: "Near the Fourth of July in a Pandemic"
The Mum Poem Press: "Sunflowers"
NELLE: "How to Wait (at the Fertility Clinic)"
North American Review: "Poem Written on the Blue Line"
Sheila-Na-Gig online: "After Quarantine, We Go Out into Marigold Light," "Asteroidea," "Fishing Lessons," "To My Daughter in the Living Room, Dancing"
The Shore: "Hope Is a Wildfire"
Sweet Lit: "After Two Years, the Midwife Explains," "Uninhabited"
SWWIM Every Day: "Cathedral," "Light Feast on the Olentangy"
Thimble Literary Magazine: "At Elyse's Baby Shower"
Voicemail Poems: "Phone Date"
West Trade Review: "The Only Constant"
Whale Road Review: "At Saint Stephen's"
Writing in a Woman's Voice: "News of the Broken World"

Chapbooks

So Much Tending Remains (Kelsay Books, 2022): "At Elyse's Baby Shower," "In a room with white walls," "Mother of Mine," "Near the Fourth of July in a Pandemic," "Sunflowers"

To Bend and Braid (Kelsay Books, 2023): "Anniversary at New River Gorge," "The Carrier," "Light Feast on the Olentangy," "On the Playground, I Think about How a Mother Is Like a Moth," "To My Daughter in the Living Room, Dancing," "Walking in the Rain I Wonder When Postpartum Depression Becomes Just Regular Depression"

Honors

Free Verse Revolution: Pushcart Prize nomination, "From Forest to Sea" (2023)

Minerva Rising Press: Pushcart Prize nomination, "On the Playground, I Think about How a Mother Is Like a Moth" (2021)

Sheila-Na-Gig online: Pushcart Prize nomination, "Fishing Lessons" (2024)

Sundress Publications: Poetry Broadside Contest Runner-up, "Fishing Lessons" (2023)

Sweet Lit: Poetry Contest finalist, "Uninhabited" (2024)

Whale Road Review: Best Spiritual Literature nomination, "At Saint Stephen's" (2023)

"The Carrier" was set to music by composer Katerina Gimon, commissioned by withonevoice, Brian J. Winnie, Artistic Director, and premiered July 2025 in Chicago and Macomb, IL.

for Saoirse

for B.

&

*for the women
upstairs in the stone church
at night*

Contents

I.

II.

III.

IV.

"You, sent out beyond your recall,
go to the limits of your longing.
Embody me."

—Rainer Maria Rilke

I.

Uninhabited

That January we ate ramen, broth sharp
as vinegar. Sipped the sizzling disappointment

while snow cascaded from the second floor
until our city grew unrecognizable. By April

love was a chore, in service of something
that wouldn't come. Spring, razor-hot July

into August—another autumn, uninhabited.
I dreamt of gardens to rip bare. I dreamt

of my childhood home, stripped of its topsoil,
three acres of mud where we planted grass

every year. In November we drove south
to the caverns of Kentucky, where the guide

clicked off her lantern, said to wave
our hands before our faces, see nothing.

Dark as ocean, blank as the black
at the center of my body—

that small cave I carried everywhere,
year into year, home to none.

Cathedral

Upstairs in the stone church
at night, we gather once each month,
and not to pray. At the center

of the table, tiny cupcakes cluster
like an offering: light pink icing,
soft blue sugar, left untouched.

Instead, a circle of stories unfolds,
each of us reciting her chapter, so often
unchanged month after month

after month. We are a chorus of grief
in metal folding chairs; we are a collective
hush: here for the holiness

of being heard, for the echoes bearing
into the emptiness like a cathedral
of children, singing.

Periphery

Remember when we pried open
oysters by the blue water, white
wine in paper cups? We had been

married seven years then.
We pulled olive bread to pieces
and talked about kids. We were

kids. It was somewhere off Highway
One, California grass wild and dry,
sky as blue as the water, almost

monochromatic. Beside the shore,
the worn path reminded me of others:
narrow boards in the Wicklow hills,

desert gravel in Nevada. So many
landscapes with you in my periphery,
with me in yours. I took a hollowed

oyster, its two shells both separate
and bound, and traced a finger across
its backs, risen like miniature mountains.

Fishing Lessons

On the dock at King Beach, my father
shows me how to pierce a nightcrawler

with a delicate hook; how to cast
the line out into the pull of the grey

wake, where boats send crimped waves
over the surface like an endless greeting;

how to wait below the bowl of an Ohio
early summer sky for a fish to bite, or not.

Just as we are about to call it, the line
catches, surprising me with its sudden

strength, and I clumsily hoist the prize:
bluegill the size of my hand, all flail and flip,

small but declared large enough to keep,
for our purposes. Which are: how to

scrape the scales away, slicing silver skin
but not your own fingers; how to smooth

back the gills like wiry feathers; and finally,
how to heat the thin filet from translucent

to white, pooled in melted butter and salt.
How to move through this world, attentive

to small tasks that make up a story, a life;
how to look closely at the work of your own

hands and call it good; how to give back
to the water when you should, but otherwise

know a keeper when you see it, then hold on
like hell with an unspoken reverence for it all.

Turning Thirty in Miami

Near Little Havana, we sat under black sky
and bougainvillea. It was December,

my birthday. It was red wine warm
in our palms, a burning in my belly

where a baby should be. It was bare feet
in the gravel garden, the dog next door

who slipped between the slats to sniff
our knees. In the morning, in the Everglades,

it was wild electric green, roaring rain
four miles out. It was watching miniature

frogs in puddles; counting gashes across
an alligator's back; fighting the downpour

with arms closed, until we didn't.
Until my hands released like a prayer

undone, cool water running over
like some kind of untamable hope.

Genesis

I could forgive the tiny garden
of bruises across my belly,

but when the kind nurse,
apologizing for cold hands,

drew two fist-sized targets
with a Sharpie above the waist

of my worn-out sweatpants,
I remembered that commandment,

unbidden: *Go forth and multiply.*
Go forth and place a needle, thick

as a dart, here or here. Go forth
and gather acrid alcohol wipes,

a cloth to catch any blood. *Be fruitful.*
Fill the earth with sons and daughters.

But what if there isn't any *dominion*
to be had—over the earth, its creatures,

beast or seed? Over my own flesh
born of *His own image*?

At the Garden Center on Mother's Day

I scan the promising packets,
so neatly cataloged in their spinners,
savoring the names I don't know
that I could ever grow, even in ideal
conditions: thick papaya seeds,
black as gems; golden kiwi; dusty blue
elderberry. Last year, even the humble
cucumber evaded me: too much light
or not enough, its failures left
unexplained in the sun-dried dirt.

See, this is what I thought it meant
to be a woman: one who bears,
not one who wants. I was taught
that sin was born of the body—hers—
eating a scarlet apple, clear juice
rivering down her chin, desire itself
a betrayal. Now I choose a sleeve
of pomegranate seeds. I'll plant
a supple forest: every fruit ripening
just out of reach.

Not Cassatt's Daughter

—after *Simone in a Blue Bonnet (No. 1)*,
Mary Cassatt, San Diego Museum of Art

Simone was not Cassatt's daughter,
so the placard tells me, and this
means her blue bonnet wasn't tied
by Mary's fingers, undoubtedly streaked
with pink and soft green—not the milk
and sweat of motherhood. Simone looks
to the side, dark-eyed, flaxen-haired
and flushed, as if she would rather
dart through fields of the Oise Valley
than have her girlish impatience rendered
in nursery hues. In the gift shop, I page
through prints replete with mothers: cheeks
curved and full, fresh as the child-dolls
they bathe or breastfeed. Their gaze,
like Simone's, directed downward,
outward, beyond—not once gracing
artist or viewer.

I Sit Among the Mothers

in the balcony, summer heat risen,
legs stuck to the pew. Cross

my hands, uncross them. Cross
myself at the altar: bread

and blood, body and wine.
Wind my way back, grief quiet

as the wafer on my tongue,
soft as a hymn hummed

by a child, unheard.

Night Class with Gonal-F

In the plastic pouch, the pen—clicking to the precise dose. In my stomach, the needle. In the bathroom stall, a narrowing— ancient door of heavy oak, etched with names I don't know. On the phone, the panic when the clicks come up short. Down the fire escape—the slick of cold black rain. On the side street where he waits, idling in the old Jeep—second pen in hand, still cool from the fridge. The twin bruises, blooming as I walk back to class. The professor's voice, unheard. In my notebook, the name I dare to write, only once.

How to Wait (at the Fertility Clinic)

First, where not to look: directly at anyone already
waiting, any woman exiting through any door.

At the oversized baby portraits lining the grey walls,
close-up of tiny tan toes, canvas catching fluorescent glare.

Next, seat yourself at least two vinyl chairs removed.[1]
Keep any accidental eye contact brief. If you must speak,

let it be only of failures in low, hushed tones. Kindly refrain
from bringing your first child, a glowing toddler, with you.[2]

Lastly, before they call your name, ask yourself how
you knew the rules[3] before you ever walked in,

before you imagined you'd be one in a roomful of women,
alone.[4]

---

[1] Optional: Glance at, but do not pick up, the outdated magazines.
[2] Do bring: Tylenol, tissues, a blank check.
[3] It will be a long time before you ask yourself why you followed
these rules, and who wrote them. When that day arrives, forgive.
[4] You are not alone.

Progesterone in Oil

This one must go into muscle.
Sometimes it brings forth blood
without warning. Propped

to one side, I press my eyes tight
as he draws viscous liquid
from a tiny vial, hands

reluctant yet steady. Afterwards,
I switch from ice to heat. Feel
the oil spread like an inner

burning. Count a heartbeat
faint as breath in my back.

Ultrasound

I was seven when the sea turned
on me, tossed me sideways, stole

    my footing, sloshed me to shore
    like a weed. I stood in saltwater,

sandy hair stuck to my shoulders,
stunned. When I saw the pearly spine

    in the ocean of my body, heard
    the static flutter, it was like that:

a grief unleashed. I said her name,
and the waves overtook me.

    What could I do but surrender
    to their swell? I shed years

of longing like an old skin,
stood reborn, then waded in.

III.

Eleven Weeks

By now, the makings
of eyes. Ten fine fingers

folded into fists. Furtive
underwater kicks. My belly

swollen from needles,
your body the size of a fig.

A friend thrums the table
at the news—*knock on wood!*—

as if every thought of you
weren't haloed with a plea—

every beat a prayer for your
soft pink heart not to leave.

Self-Portrait as Not the Giantess

—after *The Giantess (The Guardian of the Egg)*,
Leonora Carrington, 1947

I am no mother
goddess, cheeks serene
as a winter moon haloed

in gilt. Instead, at thirty weeks,
I find gold beads leaked
through my t-shirt

each morning. Like her,
I go barefoot in the late spring
heat, yet my ankles—fat and pink

among thick green—
are nothing like her slender
soles. Would the Giantess,

body a round red bell,
dare to reach for the stray piece
of violet onion on her kitchen floor?

After bathing, do her lemon
curls circle the drain in wisps?
No, despite wild geese and dark

turquoise sea, she guards her prize—
small spotted egg at her center,
perched over her heart—

with quiet assurance. This,
I realize, is what holds my gaze:
not only her vast grace,

seemingly unbothered by an egg's
breakable beginning. Perhaps
the Giantess knows

the fragility of things—and yet
she holds them lightly, holds
her whole self gently.

The Birth of Undoing

It is not morning   not winter   I am not

three centimeters   unclosed   I am not

in the right position   the midwife says

without further instruction   I am not

breathing   without an oxygen mask

not   in the bath   warm waters a cradle

for those within   I am not a voice   of stone

on stone   not weeping   from every opening

You are not   emerging   quickly enough

the resident explains   as the television plays

You are not   a heart in distress   not   not

You are not   breathing   immediately

room full of faces   ready to wake

your lungs   to life   This time

the cry   is not mine   You tear the air

I am not   only undone   I am yours

and this is the birth   of pretending

you are mine   as dawn   draws over

the world   like an eye   You open

your eyes   You are not   here   and then

you are   you are

In a room with white walls,

white floor speckled like an egg,
white sheets: you are hours old

and wrapped in a white blanket,
waking every hour to eat.

The door to our room, weighted
and thick, separates us from the rest

of the ward. Our only visitors:
nurses, midwives, and the kind

social worker, here to tell me
the signs of *more than baby blues*.

I nod, but my eyes stray to you.
I am all jubilance, distracted

by sleepless joy. Later, as the days
and nights blur, I'll remember

her words—warm as the first sip
of tea, tasting of a courage

both bitter and honeyed.

Near the Fourth of July in a Pandemic

The summer you were born, fireworks sputtered and crackled every night for weeks, briefly luminous. Roused from sleep by the weight of you, I heard them still, even as the sky blued. One hand to my belly to catch your kicks, I wondered who stayed awake lighting fuse after fuse—igniting Chrysanthemums and Catherine Wheels, ashes settling in the grass like spent confetti, beads of light growing dim against the dawn. When I finally held your body to mine, near that Fourth of July in a pandemic, I wondered how to tell you about this, the summer you were born: These months marked equally by fever and fear, a closeness heavy in the lungs, air sulfured—as well as all the joy I could bear in your brand-new eyes, two lights radiating everywhere, turning the weary world into the brightest place I'd ever dreamed.

Sunflowers

Those days were for moving thin rivers
of milk from my body to yours. Leaves,
newly golden, skidded over the pavement
like husks. I poured my morning coffee
over ice in the afternoons. Acorns clogged
the curb. I often forgot to eat, tried not to count
the purple streaks on my breasts, my back.
Clothes went unfolded. An enthusiastic cricket
got trapped somewhere in the basement.
My mind hazy as a lullaby, as if the days
were, in some ways, already memories.
In the garden off the alley we found
a patch of sunflowers by accident.
They were covered in small bees.
I tugged the thick gold petals,
then let them go. It was enough.

Mother of Mine

Her short hair shimmers across her forehead,
pearl-white as the scoop of an oyster shell.

She cares for you on Mondays and Tuesdays,
sipping black coffee that always, always,

goes cold in its cup. Upstairs, I stare
into the screen, listen to the two of you:

glee made audible in shrieks and praises,
books read in rhyming lines, the chair's

gentle creaks. You sleep. When you wake,
you might wonder after me, mostly as a body

that feeds you. I don't mind. This mother
of mine lavishes love on you in waves:

clear, cool water cascading over you,
over me—channels both known and new.

At Elyse's Baby Shower

You wake up hungry and hollering so we leave the other
guests, wandering the church basement hallway to find
an empty meeting room where I sit on a folding chair
to feed you as sunlight dyes the room gold. The carpet
is undeniably seventies, yarn-like, a potpourri palette,
and there's the smell of old books, although the shelves
are bare. I notice your hair growing lighter, catching
the sun like water, and your eyes, too, have recently
gone from navy to lake blue. It is our first October
together. Last year I was five weeks pregnant and
afraid. Now I hear Elyse in the other room, saying
thank you again and again, crumpling tissue, tearing
paper, unveiling the artifacts of new life. Now I rest
in golden light, feeding my own child, saying silently,
again and again: *Thank you thank you thank you.*

Anniversary at New River Gorge

From up here, I said, *the trees*
look like one kind of tree.

But we know better now,
which is why we can't stay here,

up on Diamond Outlook
above the grey-white water

dotted with kayaks, a state away
from our one-year-old daughter.

The gift for eleven years is steel,
bound and bonded—some kind

of testament to the strength
that brought us here intact.

What we've brought to this place
are two parts of a new whole,

two cards unwritten, an appetite
for sapphire sky—but soon

we'll have to wade back in,
back down where there is space

between the roots, both needles
and leaves and occasional petals,

pale pebbles mired in mud—
I could go on. *But isn't it amazing,*

how all the way up here,
we can still hear the rapids

calling our names?

On the Playground, I Think about How a Mother Is Like a Moth

In this bright world of play—
all blues and greens, the creak

       of swings—your laugh alights
       like dandelion seeds.

Folding your fingers
around mine, you slide

       down from the plastic perch
       with one brief shriek,

then motion for more:
again, again.

       Soon, you'll roam this place
       on your own, seek

my hands some other way,
or not at all.

       Above us in an ancient oak,
       there is a sun-bleached

kite, wings worn soft
as a moth's—

       a creature caught,
       yet willingly tethered.

Walking in the Rain I Wonder When Postpartum Depression Becomes Just Regular Depression

I picture us on a paper map, two dots
connected, gliding from block to block.

Pencil shading for some sky, square
cars tracing wide half-circles around us.

When you fall asleep I keep walking,
even as a coming storm colors the clouds,

even as bulbs of rain pool on the hood
of your stroller, slick the pavement.

I think of how it's been nearly a year
of this grey haze that fades and comes back

again. How I once thought I had to learn
to shake it, or at least to shoulder it in secret.

What I've learned instead is something like
how to walk without watching for rain.

To let go of the maps we draw for ourselves.
To let go of what we think the weather should be.

The Carrier

How sweet to drink September air,
to walk in mud and green,

you in the carrier on your father's
back. Sweet, how he gifts you

grasses wide as ribbon,
weeds that look like wheat.

Sweet, the way your eyes beam
when I turn toward the pair of you.

How sweet to carry nothing
but cool water for myself,

to walk freely and lightly, yet
beside you still. Sweet, sweet,

through forest or field, how
he knows, and can, and does,

sometimes carry us both.

After Quarantine, We Go Out into Marigold Light

in search of zinnias, faded to pink,
the last bouquet of emerald peppers.

Summer squash rotted and frozen,
pale skin crusted with ice. You say:

Let's see what we see, leading me
on thin paths crowded by dried dill,

your wonder gracing everything—
especially the pumpkins that will

never grow, green as summer,
palm-sized and already dying.

Your cough is muffled by the open
world. I can smell the air again.

I try to exhale the fears that have
flourished alongside you since

before you touched the earth.
I say it like a prayer that won't

sink in, like frost on the surface
of things: One breath, another.

These fruits don't need to be harvested.

II.

Unearthed

You are two and each day is a world
in which to peel gold pawpaw leaves

from the path; to plunk pebbles
in water, one by one; to trace tar

ribbons on cement in watermelon
rainboots, wholly unhurried,

in joyous pursuit of what it is, not
what it means, to live in this place.

I like to think I can try on your wonder,
see beyond the beauty I sift for, let

the seeing itself be the gift. I want to
remember how to attend, how to soften

even toward the fear that flows in me
like a throughline, like a frozen stream

in stone; how to imagine that what I've
buried might be worthy of this earth,

might be unearthed; how to hold it
in my hands, as gently as I hold you.

At Saint Stephen's

The communion wafer fills your whole palm.
You color over hymns with black crayon

while I squint to make out a melody, then
crawl away from me on the blonde pews—

curls soft and whirling after last night's bath,
constellation of cereal in your wake, shouting

your own invented song in perfect harmony
with yourself—and eventually, I surrender:

letting you lead me outside the glass doors,
into wild violets and uncut grass, where God is.

After this, my fantasy is

what we used to call an average Saturday night: you, me,
G&Ts at Club 185, ice singing in glass over The Black Keys on
the jukebox; candy lights and swinging my legs off the stool
like a kid. Instead, we give in, cook macaroni and cheese for
the third time this week; while our daughter eats, you rinse
dishes in water that steams your hands pink. Later when she
succumbs to sleep, I slip from her room, stand in the kitchen
holding the silence, my face in the dark window only half-
recognized—until you emerge, slicing the space between us
like a sea that reaches—somehow, perhaps even miraculously—
from there to here, then to now, you to me.

Another Ocean

As the waves recede,
you hold on to my knee,
strands of seaweed

hugging your heel,
your hair full of wind,
sand shimmering on skin.

Then you flee from me,
chasing gulls and other things
that elude my grasp.

You are water, wild
as weather—you have become
another ocean.

Soon you will sleep
in my arms under a thin towel
and seem small again.

Awash in relief, I will
watch the water turn from
aqua to navy to grey.

I will watch as a seal,
dark and elegant,
skirts the shore

with an eye toward us,
then wish you awake again
to see it.

Asteroidea

You're mine, she says, stringy arms
trapping my head to her chest.

Mine, with the certainty only a child
can summon, body stretched

over sand-colored sheets like a starfish.
When her father says *No, she belongs*

to herself, she strikes with sudden
strength, limbs curled and clinging,

and it's then that I recognize her
claim: the one that, each morning,

I don't let myself make. Prying
her arms away gently, I steady

her water-blue eyes with mine,
see the depths of us surface,

know it's true when I say
yes and *yes.*

Wild Church

At Cedar Bog, I point to marsh marigolds,
Solomon's plume—but turn to see you
gathering sugar maple pods from the path,

shucking the seed from the husk
to reveal a waxen rosary bead, green
as June. Skunk cabbage, leaves

lush and large, lovely despite its name,
stretches out like a field punctuated
by trillium. This is our cathedral, yet

even here, I am trying to hurry you,
to grasp your attention, pluck it like a stem
as if it could belong to me, and why?

Hurry toward the sedge meadow
and its silent waters, dark as tea?
Hurry, hurry to the gray rat snake,

twined in a tree to sun herself
above the creek? The unnameable
beckons in all forms, yet the rush runs

through me—unwilling to ebb until
it isn't, until I remember that such
stillness was meant for me, too.

Mother of Nations

—after "Sarah," *Mothers of the Bible* series,
Henry Ossawa Tanner, 1902

*That in her were found all the virtues of a true mother can be
judged from the fact that the one sorrow of her life was that she
was childless . . .*

Sarah beside the spindle—pale arms poised
as a dancer's; her son at her feet, attentive.
The woven mats swept to order.
Her expression calmly adoring, only

a little tired. Nothing suggests earlier shadows,
seemingly buried by bliss. Nothing suggests
her sorrow still lives in her, surprising her
when her son wanders too far into forest;

blazing into being when her husband,
devoted and foolish, nearly burns it all
to ash. Their long-awaited lamb.
What kind of God gives then takes?

What kind of God never gives at all?
She thinks of the old woman at the well,
how she looked at Isaac when he was small
yet never found Sarah's eyes. What kind of God?

These are the questions Sarah won't ask.
Shadows at the edge of a careful composition.
She has her answer, doesn't she? Yet
she also has her sorrows. What kind

of woman contains only singularities?

Tributary

—for Maxine "Maukie" Patterson, 1934–2019

For ten days I watched the bones
of your hands shimmer through your skin
{blue yet soft as breath}

> For ten years I copied you in kitchens,
> breathing over a boiling pot
> to temper its brimming

Nineteen when we met, you
taught me as a grandmother does,
even then {iron hissing

> over crisp shirts,
> cucumbers sliced to wet coins,
> rainbow of zinnias gathered in jars}

For ten days the oxygen thrummed
by your bedside {at your window,
snow turned to water on the pane}

> Rivers torn and meeting again,
> one silent streaming song
> feeding another {then and now}

To My Daughter in the Living Room, Dancing

I've never been good at it—
the dancing or the surrender,

>   but you are insistent: curls
>   stretched to wild waves

that stream behind your blur
of a body, shrieks clear

>   as the cold rain making rivers
>   on the window, where surely

the neighbors spot me swaying,
grinning at you below the pane.

>   We dance anyway—hands joined
>   to twirl with reckless delight,

and I think of how my mother
once said that joy is more

>   powerful than sorrow. How
>   I didn't believe her. And yet.

The Only Constant

The thing is, it's Sunday, and by nine,
we're already three *Sesame Street*
episodes in when it begins to snow,
fat flakes falling fast. It takes at least
forty-five minutes to gather two coats
each, your hot-pink snow pants,
and only one mitten. I can reach
your red plastic sled from the rafters,
but when you realize you can't ride
and pull yourself all at once, it's over—
sled left to gather ice in the street.
Instead we shake puffs of snow
from the hydrangeas, watch them
spring up like a release. The thing is,
my patience lately seems to have
died, its once plush petals hardened
yet fragile, buried under winter
weight. I cannot seem to follow
the advice—to remain unfazed
as you scream when I won't let you
eat the snow from your boots,
when you push your will against mine
only to pivot to need, to me—our bodies
once again a connected heap. Later,
I scald the grilled cheese, scrape its burnt
into the sink. You tell me the inside
is best anyway, carefully peeling
a stretch of cheddar from the crust.
The thing is, you forgive me constantly:
missing mittens, blackened bread,
the edge in my voice that reveals
too much, the way I am still learning
how to forgive myself.

The First Time I Heard Your Separate Song

This year, there aren't enough wings
to go around. But you have a headband

wrapped with glitter garland, white dress
over white tights, toes in too-small slippers.

On stage you are still and not singing;
I lean forward in the pew, poised to pluck

you from the scene should the *joy
to the world* become too much.

As your forehead softens, I sit back,
remember to glance at the hymnal,

look elsewhere—at the other kids,
shepherds with sheets tied to their heads;

the wreath with its pink and violet tapers;
everything agleam against a cardboard curtain

painted navy, misshapen star at its crown.
As the nave goes dark, you remain in place;

I hold the glow of a candle alongside
my quiet disbelief, and wonder

where the line went—the one between
the anticipation of your needs and my own

desires. I watch the warm wax slip
from the flame, then catch you

pulling your halo off, peering
at the doll in its makeshift manger,

and realize I'm the one holding still,
holding on—my whole body humming

as you begin to sing your separate song.

After Two Years, the Midwife Explains

pre{*eclampsia*—a condition comparable
to *milk fever*
in cows and dogs}

which explains
how my blood soared in the days after
as drops of milk rivered

how my fingers blushed and bore
red rings, even after
the silver was cut from my hand

{from the Greek *éklampsis*,
a violent onset} which explains
the lack of time—

{*pre-*, as in earlier than}
—the body no longer safe
to hold another's

which explains three centimeters
to nine {*eklámpein*,
to burst forth}

the suddenness of dark
to dawn {*lámpein*,
to shine out}

the bloom of my daughter's night-
blue eyes bearing so much
light

which might explain—I don't say—
how the body glows
{even now}

IV.

Poem Written on the Blue Line

We are good pretenders: not holding
the handrail too tightly; maintaining

a practiced boredom as the train curves,
stops, starts again; passing through turnstiles

with calculated ease to emerge into Midtown.
There's no snow, bricks still littered with gold

ginkgoes, but there's a rink in Central Park
where kids trace circles on the ice.

We complain the leaves are out of place;
we want to look like tourists who are maybe

not tourists, but now we're in Macy's
in the middle of the day not buying

anything. Still, we think we've got it when
someone asks for directions, which line to take

to Fort Green, that same nonchalance
in their voice that says, *We don't belong here*

but could. This time, though, we sense a shift:
We are not only possibilities, but rooted in a place

that isn't here. Back in Ohio, our daughter
runs circles around a fir tree too big for the room,

its branches skirting the ceiling. We hear her call
over the city's roar, a pull as unstoppable as the train

we just missed. There's another one coming
in six minutes, headed west—and we'll be on it.

News of the Broken World

arrives on our front porch in the image
of a woman, pregnant, body and clothes aglow

against the maternity center blasted by bombs,
her child sheltered by her body, her body

unsheltered, her world a shell, shelled.

My own daughter wakes up fevered, vomits
milk and mucus beneath the kitchen table,

and so I keep her home, keep her close,
sick and safe as she sleeps outside my body,

inside these unbruised walls. Hours later,

awake and alight at the window, we watch
the stillness of our neighbors' houses,

clustered and intact; weak sunlight in a sky
absent of any threat—this earth untouched

by ashes and audacious enough to bloom.

Witness

My daughter wakes
but doesn't wake, words
lost to the dark that floods

the room, terror tossing
wave after wave over
her small body.

At the shore of her
shadowed sleep, I can only
witness her wading

through, the way I stayed
as my sister bore
her own child

into this world, wet lungs
lurching then catching
on air—breathing

her way into being.
As my daughter struggles
toward and away

from me, I think of how
sometimes being is the only
doing we have,

and how often I have raged
against this—a truth
too much to bear

and yet. It's not enough
to sing her back to me,
but I sing anyway:

I am here I am
here I am
here.

Notes on *Love of a Child, Being a Parent*

—Judy Drew, charcoal on paper

I.

First, it's the mother's brow that gets me:
full and deep, more than a furrow—
like a child presses crayon to paper,

hand in fist—the word I hold
in my mouth, unsaid,
is *fraught*

with memory and meaning {from
frawten, a carrier in unknown
waters, so laden she can hardly sail}

II.

Then, her arms—how one bears
her child's full weight, the other pressing in
as if willing this heavy closeness to remain

　　　　And I remember all my body could not do—
　　　　how I could not carry her down stairs,
　　　　over concrete, near water—

how the freight stayed with me {*frêht:*
a reward, a recompense}—how I carried it
even as I carried her

III.

Now my eyes stray to the unsteady edges,
the blurred blankness beyond their faces
in stark unfinished lines

> Now I want only to reconcile myself
> to myself—to carry {*carier, charier:*
> to transport, to bear}

every mother in me

Light Feast on the Olentangy

The river's edge teems with leafy
groundcover, tiny forest
that steals the sound from our steps.

In its lushness, you stumble silently
in search of stems that glow. Soon
you turn toward me again, yellow petals

starring your chin, stems in your hand
reduced to their centers—and really,
I can understand why you'd want

to consume their color, to get close
to that wild beauty, to know it
in a whole-bodied way. Later

when you lie on the grass, twigs
catching in your curls, I do the same:
watching you watch the branches

etch a web against the pale sky. At least,
this is what I think you see, but perhaps
it's pinecones, or the wind, or something

unknowable in your growing mind.
In my own mind I wonder how we
got here, how once my body carried

yours, but now your wonder
enfolds us both, opens me up each
morning like a field feasting on light.

After Visiting the Pacific Island Water Garden

I.

It should be magical:
syrupy air, koi lazing
in dark pools, a forest
of ferns, and above, around, abounding:

Emerald Swallowtails,
Julia Longwings (tangerine
bright), Mexican Sisters,
Cattlehearts (stained glass at night).

We watch them sip beads from waxen leaves.
You will the wings to your palm
like I coax you toward the path
(yet we, too, flit erratically).

Near a pair of Blue Morphos,
a small boy approaches,
then (wordlessly)
slaps your face.

II.

Some butterflies forego fragile
blooms in favor of (rotted) fruit.
Most live only two weeks.

I think of taking the slap
into my own body, my stomach
(sour as a stone, pitted).

The overripe juices
of a browning peach shouldn't shock me,
I know.

But I am still mourning the delicate world
and the one I wanted
for you.

Phone Date

On Sunday—sheets stripped,
bed bare, afternoon edging toward
gold—my sister picks up

on speaker phone. As she feeds
her brand-new daughter—
backdrop all static and shift,

a chorus of coos until, suddenly,
that hush of relief—my own child
emerges with wordless urgency

to show me the split in her fingernail,
pink and soft as a shell
tossed to shore. I take her hand,

try to smooth what is sharp—
as so many women before us
have done, yet knowing each mother

must learn this for herself.
Still, I cradle the phone
between cheek and shoulder

to catch my sister's half-formed
sentences, my niece's chirps
and starts—until my daughter

frees her hand, skips away
singing. Until light breaks through
the blinds, fills the whole room.

Language of the Birds

On the patio, you paint terra-cotta
pots laden with last year's dirt,
dipping the thin brush into a cup
of grey water to render shadow
pictures on the clay. I watch
as they turn from rust to brown
and back. It is nearly May, green
deepening between the houses
stacked in rows. You are nearly
three, folding your body over
the brick wall to send dandelion seeds
into an ocean of rocks below,
where my eye catches on unwanted
clover and wild strawberry
vining the edge of the fence.
I think of pulling them to the roots
but don't. I think of braiding
the uncut grass. Then I begin
to see: Those petals you've piled
on the pathway? Forest confetti.
That song you shout as you plant
pebbles in the pots, seeds snagged
in your hair like miniature feathers?
Language of the birds, hymn
of your own making, each note
bringing you deeper toward
yourself.

After My Daughter's First Week of Preschool

I.

Like a branch nearly severed,
the deer's antler—a dead thing,

a cord cut—no longer points
toward sky, its bloody velvet

dangling beside a round eye
that catches mine, then steadies.

At first, I imagine his distress,
until I remember: This loss

is simply the way of things.
Regular as the leaving

of birds before winter.

II.

That night as my daughter sleeps,
I search *do deer feel pain when*—

trying to map a metaphor that isn't
mine. I learn this: In the second phase

of a fawn's life, they are often alone
in the tall grass. The doe knows

that separation is part of mothering.
But isn't absence another word

for loss? Does the mother
feel the lack, and for how long?

are inquiries that yield no results.
My daughter shifts but doesn't wake,

grows deeper toward unseen dreams.

Hope Is a Wildfire

When Canada sends down
its curtain of smoke—rending
the ripe June air,

the sun a smudged coin—
night comes sooner
to my daughter's window.

Rocking her to sleep
in the thick haze of heat,
I think of how some things

only dissipate when you
get close—and that's a story
I want to tell her, to tell myself,

even though the forests
are still burning down
while the sea level rises.

Even though the sparrow,
one wing bent, shuddered
and died on our own porch.

There are so many songs
of loss I've yet to sing—
their weight clouding

my vision. Night wings
toward morning—I rise
to its music, even though.

Cape Elizabeth

is cloudless, wind whirling our hair into tangles; is seagrass
giving in to dark water, blue in every direction; is lobsters
pulled to pieces on paper placemats. Cape Elizabeth is us, ten
years ago, stepping over these same rocks; is now, is you,
three years old at the bright red picnic table, heaps of crinkled
fries clustered in your fist as you grin. Cape Elizabeth is cups
of clam chowder, thin onion rings, cold pickle coins; is salt on
our tongues; is your small hands in ours as we climb; is tide
pools caught between boulders; is an ocean unspooled, made
familiar and new.

From Forest to Sea

I point to lichen like lace on the pitch pines,
but you don't need me to teach you

how to move through this world
in search of beauty. You are in search

of everything, equally: dull limestone,
pinecones plentiful as berries,

the spider's delicate legs.
On the path from forest to sea,

your endless curiosity slows our steps,
your pace propelled by wonder, not

destination. Near the shoreline,
I bend to touch the sand as you do,

to trace the letters you know, then
let the surf have them back—

as if something finished weren't
the point of it, but rather something

seen and held, however briefly.

Cadence

The second night at Blackwoods, we talk over nearby fires snapping sparks while our daughter sleeps in the dark pocket of the tent. In the wedge of black between branches: uncountable stars. Beyond the thin strip of forest: a map that stops, goes blue. All day, we tried to stay above water. All day, I thought of us and not us: the ones who slept deeply in the desert for days, who ran miles through Ohio forests, who stood inside clouds on Croagh Patrick and the hollow caves of Kentucky. The pace that pulls at us now washes over the weight of our earlier selves. But here, the night waves offer their refrain: Tomorrow remains uncharted, a chance to stop our plans, to throw clumps of sopping sand. To collect dark mussels at low tide, marvel at bright lichen on the boulders. To inhabit the cadence of this shared, ever-changing song.

About the Author

Emily Patterson's poetry appears in *Christian Century, SWWIM Every Day, North American Review, CALYX, The Penn Review, Cordella Magazine, NELLE,* and elsewhere. She is the author of three chapbooks, including *So Much Tending Remains* (Kelsay Books, 2022), *To Bend and Braid* (Kelsay Books, 2023), and *haiku at 5:38 a.m.* (Bottlecap Press, 2024). Her work has been recognized and honored by Sundress Publications, *Sweet Lit,* and *Whale Road Review,* and her poem "Small is the Seed" (*Tyger Tyger Magazine,* 2024) was set to music by composer Katerina Gimon and premiered at Carnegie Hall in 2025. Emily received her B.A. in English from Ohio Wesleyan University, where she was awarded the Marie Drennan Prize for Poetry, and her M.A. in Education from The Ohio State University. She is a curriculum designer for Highlights for Children and lives with her family in Columbus, Ohio. Read more at emilypattersonpoet.com.